We wish you a
ristmas...

OXFORD
UNIVERSITY PRESS

Great Clarendon Street, Oxford OX2 6DP

Oxford University Press is a department of the University of Oxford.
It furthers the University's objective of excellence in research, scholarship,
and education by publishing worldwide in

Oxford New York

Auckland Bangkok Buenos Aires
Cape Town Chennai Dar es Salaam Delhi Hong Kong Istanbul
Karachi Kolkata Kuala Lumpur Madrid Melbourne Mexico City Mumbai
Nairobi São Paulo Shanghai Taipei Tokyo Toronto

Oxford is a registered trade mark of Oxford University Press
in the UK and in certain other countries

British Library Cataloguing in Publication Data available

ISBN 0-19-276298-2 (Hardback)
ISBN 0-19-276299-0 (Paperback)

1 3 5 7 9 10 8 6 4 2

Typeset by Mary Tudge (Typesetting Services)
in Fontoon and Old Style 7.

Printed in China

My First Oxford Book of Christmas poems

compiled by
John foster

OXFORD
UNIVERSITY PRESS

Contents

Christmas is coming...

Deck the halls with sprays of holly...

The night before Christmas...

On Christmas day, on Christmas day...

We three kings of Orient are...

Christmas is coming...

Sir Winter

I heard Sir Winter coming.
He crept out of his bed
and rubbed his thin and freezing hands:
'I'll soon be up!' he said.

'I'll shudder at the keyhole
and rattle at the door,
I'll strip the trees of all their leaves
and strew them on the floor.

'I'll harden every puddle
that Autumn thinks is his—
I'll lay a sparkling quilt of snow
on everything that is!

'I'll bring a load of darkness
as large as any coal,
and drive my husky dogs across
the world from pole to pole.

'Oho! How you will shiver!'
—And then I heard him say:
'But in the middle of it all
I'll give you
       CHRISTMAS DAY!'

Jean Kenward

Robin

Where have the birds gone
one by one?
Off to the south
and after the sun.

Only the robin,
with breast of red,
hops in the garden
and cocks his head,

fluffs up his feathers
and flits to the sill,
pecking up crumbs
as the air grows chill.

Tony Mitton

December

All the months go past
  Each is like a guest;
December is the last,
  December is the best.

Each has lovely things,
  Each one is a friend,
But December brings
  Christmas at the end.

Rose Fyleman

13

Chill December ·

Chill December brings the sleet,
Blazing fire, and Christmas treat.

Sara Coleridge

A Jewel Day

O children, wake, for a fairy world
Is waiting for you and me,
With gems aglow on the meadow grass,
And jewels on every tree.

The hedgerows glitter, the dark woods shine
In dresses of sparkling white
For while we slumbered the Ice Queen passed
All over the earth last night.

Lucy Diamond

The Snow

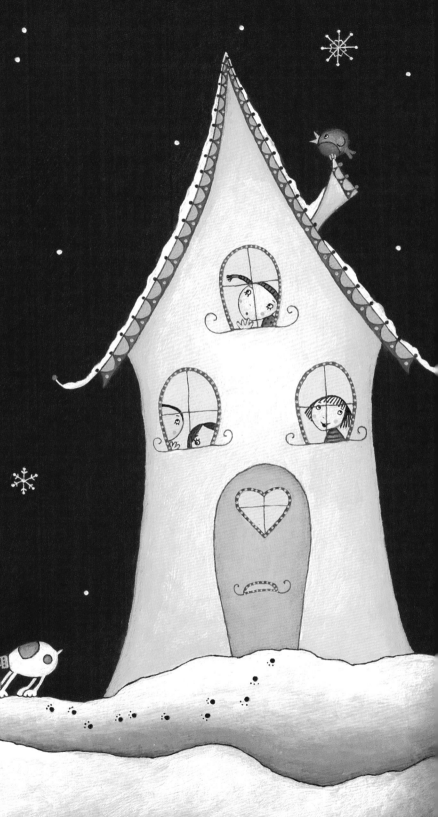

The snow, in bitter cold
    Fell all night;
And we awoke to see
    The garden white.

And still the silvery flakes
    Go whirling by,
White feathers fluttering
    From a grey sky.

Beyond the gate, soft feet
    In silence go,
Beyond the frosted pane
    White shines the snow.

F. Ann Elliott

The More It Snows

The more it
SNOWS-tiddley-pom,
The more it
GOES-tiddley-pom,
The more it
GOES-tiddley-pom
On
Snowing.

And nobody
KNOWS-tiddley-pom,
How cold my
TOES-tiddley-pom,
How cold my
TOES-tiddley-pom,
Are
Growing.

A. A. Milne

Advent Calendar

Open the window.
What do you see?
A sprig of holly
A Christmas tree
Reindeer
Santa's sleigh
Mistletoe
A snowy day
A robin redbreast
A blazing fire
Christmas cards
A church choir
A box of crackers
A frozen pond
A Christmas cake
A fairy with a wand
A big parcel
A chocolate bar
A Christmas pudding
A toy car
An angel
A shining star
Shepherds on a hillside
A stable bare
Three wise men worshipping
The baby lying there.

John Foster

22

7

8

23

Christmas Cards

Everyone is on the move
On Christmas cards;
Skaters gliding over rivers
The frost has frozen hard,
Kings with golden crowns
Riding their camels towards a star,
Even mice on their sledges
Wearing woolly hats and scarves;
Men in stovepipe hats and long thick coats
Plough a passage through the drifts
In an old-fashioned coach;
Cats sitting in the window
Look out at them in the snow
And robins in holly bushes
Watch them go.
Reindeer whirl Santa Claus
Through a gap in the clouds,
Round and round the chimneys
Towards the roof of our house.

Stanley Cook

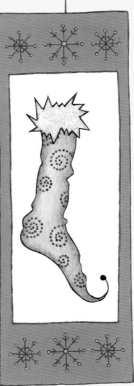

18

Parcels

How grand to hear the postman's knock
Upon the door at eight o'clock,
For surely what I like the most
Is getting parcels through the post.

Parcels tied with yards of string
And my name in large lettering;
Parcels with ten stamps or so,
All in a multi-coloured row.

Parcels thoughtful people send
Labelled *Fragile, Do Not Bend*;
Parcels every size and shape,
Sealed with wax and sticky tape.

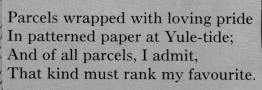

Parcels wrapped with loving pride
In patterned paper at Yule-tide;
And of all parcels, I admit,
That kind must rank my favourite.

Colin West

Waiting for Christmas

I'm waiting for Christmas;
the days dawdle by,
but the Christmas tree's up,
(easily two metres high)
all covered in tinsel
and glittering lights.
It's all too exciting;
I can't sleep at night.
My big Advent calendar's
practically through
and I can't wait much longer,
but what can I do?
I've written to Santa
(a very long list)
then wrote once again
with the things I had missed.
We've had the school party,
I've sent all my cards,
and I've hung up my stocking
but the waiting is hard.
I'm listening for sleigh bells.
I'm yearning for snow,
I'm watching the clock;
it is certainly slow.
'How many days now?'
I keep asking Mum,
then go back to waiting
for Christmas to come.

Marian Swinger

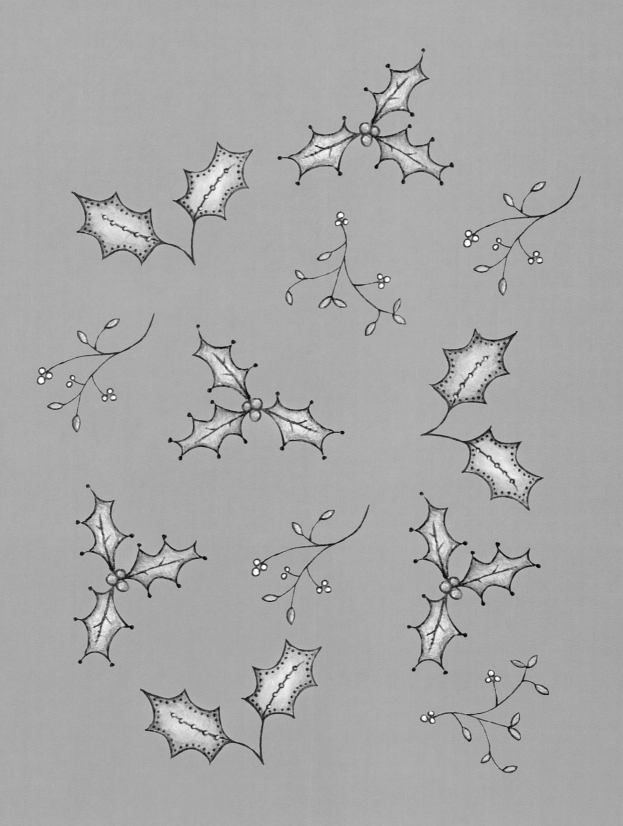

Deck the halls with sprays of holly...

School Carol

Deck the classrooms now with holly,
Christmas time has just begun.
Here's a reason to be jolly,
No more lessons, lots more fun!
Christmas cards and Christmas pictures
Are the order of the day;
Let us paint a red-nosed reindeer
Pulling Santa on his sleigh.

Deck the classrooms now with streamers,
Thread some snow of cotton-wool,
Spray a snow scene on the windows,
Make some crackers we can pull.
Decorate the tree with tinsel
Green and silver, red and gold,
Sew a needle-case for Grandma,
Soon the secrets can be told.

Deck the halls with sprays of holly,
Dress up in your party gear.
Here's a reason to be jolly,
No more lessons till next year!
Hurry to the Christmas Disco,
Come along and join the fun—
Dance and swing, and sing together:
Happy Christmas, everyone!

June Crebbin

Nativity Play

This year . . .
This year can I be Herod?
This year, can I be him?
A wise man
or a Joseph?
An inn man
or a king?

This year . . .
can I be famous?
This year, can I be best?
Bear a crown of silver
and wear a golden vest?

This year . . .
can I be starlight?
This year, can I stand out? . . .
Feel the swish of curtains
and hear the front row shout
'Hurrah' for good old Ronny
he brings a gift of gold
head afire with tinsel
'The Greatest Story Told . . .'
'Hurrah for good old Herod!'
and shepherds from afar.

So—
don't make me a palm tree
And can I be—
                    a Star?

Peter Dixon

No Room

In our old school hall,
At the end of the day,
The infants put on
Their Nativity play.

They spoke their lines clear.
They spoke their lines loud.
The parents all sat there,
Pleased, looking proud.

Mary looked holy.
The sheep made a din.
Then Joseph announced:
'There's no room at the inn.'

At that, from the hall,
Audience one quiet mouse,
Came little John's offer:
'You can stay at our house!'

John Kitching

Christmas Tree

Star over all
Eye of the night
Stand on my tree
Magical sight
Green under frost
Green under snow
Green under tinsel
Glitter and glow
Appled with baubles
Silver and gold
Spangled with fire
Warm over cold.

Laurence Smith

28

Christmas Trees

The Christmas trees in the forest
Stand in a long row,
Spreading their branches like arms
To catch the falling snow.

Their branches point at the moon
And the stars in the sky
And reach to catch the clouds
That go floating by.

When they come indoors
They gather in their arms
Christmas presents and tinsel
And hold bright lights and stars.

Stanley Cook

The Children's Carol

Here we come again, again, and here we come again!
Christmas is a single pearl swinging on a chain,
Christmas is a single flower in a barren wood,
Christmas is a single sail on the salty flood,
Christmas is a single star in the empty sky,
Christmas is a single song sung for charity.
Here we come again, again, to sing to you again,
Give a single penny that we may not sing in vain.

Eleanor Farjeon

Carol Singers

Hold the pages steady.
I want to see the notes.
Hear the voices rising
From our Christmas throats.

Singing Christmas carols
Just a trifle flat.
Surely good King Wenceslas
Would not be pleased with that.

I wish you'd try to concentrate
And make a sweeter sound.
Remember, shepherds watched their flocks
All seated on the ground.

Please do all start together
And try to get it right.
Why do you sing 'Noël, Noël'
When I sing 'Silent Night'?

How tunefully the church bells chime
Across the listening town.
Try 'Good King Wenceslas' . . . This time
He may be looking down.

Max Fatchen

31

Carole Carroll

When Carole Carroll's carol-singing
Carole Carroll's carols,
Carole's carols sound so bad
That people hide in barrels,
Yes, people run and block their ears
And hide away in barrels
When Carole Carroll's carol-singing
Carole Carroll's carols.

Richard Edwards

Mincemeat

Sing a song of mincemeat,
Currants, raisins, spice,
Apples, sugar, nutmeg,
Everything that's nice,
Stir it with a ladle,
Wish a lovely wish,
Drop it in the middle
Of your well-filled dish,
Stir again for good luck,
Pack it all away
Tied in little jars and pots,
Until Christmas day.

Elizabeth Gould

The Christmas Pudding

Into the basin
put the plums,
stir-about, stir-about,
stir-about.

Next the good
white flour comes,
stir-about, stir-about,
stir-about.

Sugar and peel
and eggs and spice,
stir-about, stir-about,
stir-about.

Mix them and fix them
and cook them twice,
stir-about, stir-about,
stir-about.

Anon.

The Christmas Pudding—from Start to Finish!

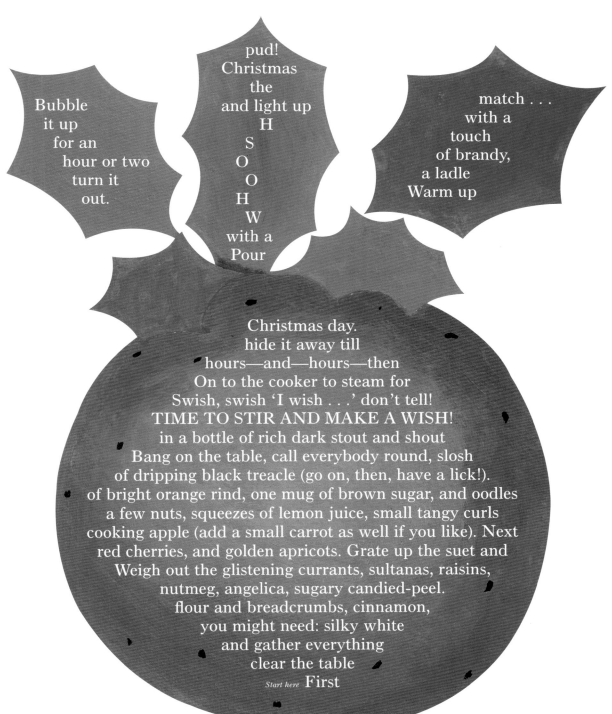

Bubble (leaf)
Bubble
it up
for an
hour or two
turn it
out.

Christmas pud! (leaf)
pud!
Christmas
the
and light up
H
S
O
O
H
W
with a
Pour

match . . . (leaf)
match . . .
with a
touch
of brandy,
a ladle
Warm up

Pudding body:
Christmas day.
hide it away till
hours—and—hours—then
On to the cooker to steam for
Swish, swish 'I wish . . .' don't tell!
TIME TO STIR AND MAKE A WISH!
in a bottle of rich dark stout and shout
Bang on the table, call everybody round, slosh
of dripping black treacle (go on, then, have a lick!).
of bright orange rind, one mug of brown sugar, and oodles
a few nuts, squeezes of lemon juice, small tangy curls
cooking apple (add a small carrot as well if you like). Next
red cherries, and golden apricots. Grate up the suet and
Weigh out the glistening currants, sultanas, raisins,
nutmeg, angelica, sugary candied-peel.
flour and breadcrumbs, cinnamon,
you might need: silky white
and gather everything
clear the table
Start here First

Patricia Leighton

H is for holly with berries red bright

R is for reindeer who stand in the snow

I is for icing with silvery glow

S is for Santa who comes very late

Brenda Williams

is for tree that stands tall and straight

is for mincepies I have for tea

is for stocking I open at dawn

is coming
The day Christ was born.

Christmas is coming

December 19

The day after the day after tomorrow
I will then be able to say
That the day after the day after that
Is the day before Christmas Day.

Steve Turner

Coming for Christmas

The Christmas star
    brings us from near and far.

We come
    on buses, bikes,
    in present-piled-high cars.

We come on trains,
    make surprise trips:
    'Won't they be amazed
    when they see who it is!'

One star—a compass
    steering us
    by ways of love
    to families and friends.

Patricia Leighton

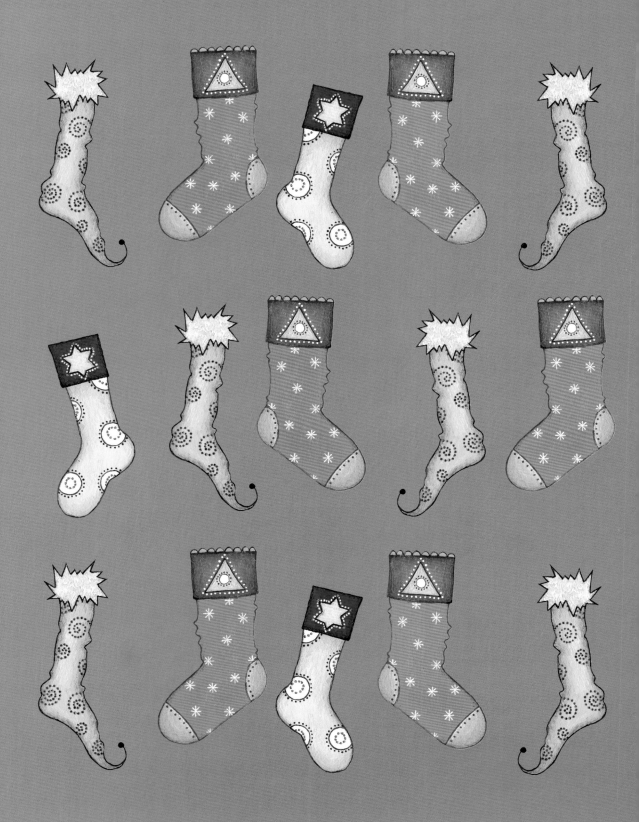

The night before Christmas...

The Snow Lies White on Roof and Tree

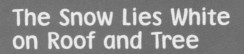

The snow lies white on roof and tree,
Frost fairies creep about,
The world's as still as it can be,
And Santa Claus is out.

He's making haste his gifts to leave,
While the stars show his way,
There'll soon be no more Christmas Eve,
Tomorrow's Christmas Day!

Anon.

Reindeer Rap

Well, it's Christmas Eve,
December 24th,
And we're on our way down
From the far, far north.
We got Santa in the sleigh
With a load of Christmas cheer,
We'll deliver the presents
Santa's worked on all year,
So if you think you hear a noise
When you're tucked up in bed,
A sorta scritch-scritch-scratching
Up above your head,
If you hear somebody tapping
Way up there on your roof
It'll just be the pawing
Of a reindeer hoof!
We'll be rapping on the rooftop,
We'll be rapping on the floor,
We'll be rapping on the window,
We'll be rapping on the door!
It's no problem towing Santa
Through the dark and snowy skies

But when he's drinking sherry wine
And eating all those mince pies
We get bored and lonely
And we wanna let him know
There's still a job to do—
Hey, man, we really gotta go!
No offence to all you people,
Just a word in your ear—
Maybe you could leave some carrots
For his cool REIN-DEER!
Or
We'll be rapping on the rooftop,
We'll be rapping on the floor,
We'll be rapping on the window,
We'll be rapping on the DOOR!

Sue Cowling

Pilot

If I could be a pilot
Each Christmas Eve I'd fly
To fetch a fluffy snow cloud
From the distant Arctic sky,
I'd chase it, catch it, tow it home
And tie it to a tree,
So snow would fall on Christmas Day
On all my friends and me.

Richard Edwards

If I Were Father Christmas

If I were Father Christmas
I'd deliver all my toys
By rocket ship, a sleigh's too slow
For eager girls and boys,
I'd nip down every chimney-pot
And never miss a roof,
While Rudolf worked the ship's controls
With antler tip and hoof.

Richard Edwards

Snuggling Down

Snow on Christmas Eve—
in the morning we may see
hoofprints on our roof.

Frances Nagle

A Visit from St Nicholas

'Twas the night before Christmas, when all through the house
Not a creature was stirring, not even a mouse;
The stockings were hung by the chimney with care,
In hopes that St Nicholas soon would be there;
The children were nestled all snug in their beds,
While visions of sugarplums danced in their heads;

And Mamma in her 'kerchief, and I in my cap,
Had just settled our brains for a long winter's nap;
When out on the lawn there arose such a clatter,
I sprang from the bed to see what was the matter.
Away to the window I flew like a flash,
Tore open the shutters and threw up the sash.

The moon, on the breast of the new-fallen snow,
Gave the lustre of midday to objects below,
When what to my wondering eyes should appear,
But a miniature sleigh, and eight tiny reindeer,
With a little old driver, so lively and quick,
I knew in a moment it must be St Nick.

More rapid than eagles his coursers they came,
And he whistled and shouted, and called them by name:
'Now, Dasher! Now, Dancer! Now, Prancer and Vixen!
On, Comet! On, Cupid! On, Donner and Blitzen!
To the top of the porch! To the top of the wall!
Now, dash away! Dash away! Dash away all!'

As dry leaves that before the wild hurricane fly,
When they meet with an obstacle, mount to the sky;
So up to the housetop the coursers they flew,
With the sleigh full of toys, and St Nicholas, too.
And then, in a twinkling, I heard on the roof
The prancing and pawing of each little hoof—
As I drew in my head, and was turning around,
Down the chimney St Nicholas came with a bound.

He was dressed all in fur, from his head to his foot,
And his clothes were all tarnished with ashes and soot;
A bundle of toys he had flung on his back,
And he looked like a pedlar just opening his pack.
His eyes—how they twinkled! His dimples, how merry!
His cheeks were like roses, his nose like a cherry!

His droll little mouth was drawn up like a bow,
And the beard of his chin was as white as the snow;
The stump of a pipe he held tight in his teeth,
And the smoke it encircled his head like a wreath;
He had a broad face and a little round belly
That shook, when he laughed, like a bowl full of jelly.

He was chubby and plump, a right jolly old elf,
And I laughed, when I saw him, in spite of myself;
A wink of his eye and a twist of his head,
Soon gave me to know I had nothing to dread;
He spoke not a word, but went straight to his work,
And filled all the stockings; then turned with a jerk,

And laying his finger aside of his nose,
And giving a nod, up the chimney he rose;
He sprang to his sleigh, to his team gave a whistle,
And away they all flew like the down of a thistle.
But I heard him exclaim, ere he drove out of sight,
'Happy Christmas to all, and to all a good night.'

Clement C. Moore

Christmas Star

There rose a star of burnished gold,
It moved with purpose through the sky,
It carried tidings yet untold,
And watchers gazed as it passed by,
Through mists of day and shadowed night,
It filled the sky with burning light.

Theresa Heine

Angels

Earth and sky,
sky and earth,
both embrace
the holy birth.

Picture angels
in that sky.
Imagine angels,
there, on high.

Angels wrapped
in angel light.
Angel music
fills the night.

Ann Bonner

48

High in the Heaven

High in the Heaven
A gold star burns
Lighting our way
As the great world turns.

Silver the frost
It shines on the stem
As we now journey
To Bethlehem.

White is the ice
At our feet as we tread,
Pointing a path
To the manger-bed.

Charles Causley

The Sky is Black Tonight

The sky is black tonight;
Coal-black, crow-black,
But in that black
Is the white-bright light
Of a star.

That star has a gift tonight:
A birth-gift, a for-all-the-earth gift.
For in that star
Is a fly-by-night:
Is a bird.

That bird has a song tonight:
A love-song, high-above song.
And in that song
Is the silver tongue
Of a bell.

That bell has a wish tonight;
A bell-wish, a well-wish.
And the wish
In the bell
In the song
In the bird
In the star
In the black
In the sky
Is Peace,
Is Peace,
Is Peace.

Berlie Doherty

The Oxen

Christmas Eve, and twelve of the clock.
'Now they are all on their knees,'
An elder said, as we sat in a flock,
By the embers in fireside ease.

We pictured the meek mild creatures, where
They dwelt in their strawy pen,
Nor did it occur to one of us there
To doubt they were kneeling then.

So fair a fancy few would weave
In these years! Yet, I feel
If someone said, on Christmas Eve,
'Come; see the oxen kneel

'In the lonely barton by yonder coomb,
Our childhood used to know,'
I should go with him in the gloom,
Hoping it might be so.

Thomas Hardy

You at Christmas

You helped to mix the Christmas cake.
The stirring made your tired arms ache.

You hung the baubles on the tree
till it was glorious to see.

You set the crib out on the shelf
and put the baby in yourself.

You helped to hang the Christmas cards.
It seemed that there were yards and yards.

And, when it came to Christmas eve,
you whispered, 'Yes, I do believe.'

With great excitement in your head
you placed your stocking by your bed.

Then, switching off your bedroom light,
you turned to view the winter night.

And what you saw there caught your eyes
and made you startle with surprise.

No jolly Santa in his sleigh
with reindeer cantering away.

But just a star so silver bright
it seemed to fill the world with light.

And, though so distant in the blue,
it hung and sparkled there for You.

Tony Mitton

Christmas Eve

Nearly midnight;
still can't sleep!
Has he been yet?
Dare I peep?

Sneak out softly,
creaking floor!
Down the stairs
and through the door…
In the darkness
by the tree,
tightly wrapped…
but which for me?

Feel the ribbon,
find the card!
This one? That one?
Heart thumps hard.
Trembling fingers,
throbbing head,
then…

a voice yells

'BACK TO BED!'

Judith Nicholls

On
Christmas
day, On
Christmas
day...

Candles

Candles waver by the window,
whisper to a wintry dawn:
Dance with us, the world is waking,
Christmas Day has come!

Candles flicker in the stable,
burn the darkness from the night:
Dance with us around this Christchild
veiled in brightness, swathed in light.

Judith Nicholls

Christmas Bells

I heard the bells on Christmas Day
Their old familiar carols play,
   And wild and sweet
   The words repeat
Of Peace on earth, Goodwill to men!

Henry Wadsworth Longfellow

Christmas Morn

Shall I tell you what will come
to Bethlehem on Christmas morn,
who will kneel them gently down
before the Lord new-born?

One small fish from the river,
with scales of red, red gold,
one wild bee from the heather,
one grey lamb from the fold,
one ox from the high pasture,
one black bull from the herd,
one goatling from the far hills,
one white, white bird.

And many children—God give them grace,
bringing tall candles to light Mary's face.

Ruth Sawyer

Long, Long Ago

Winds through the olive trees
Softly did blow,
Round little Bethlehem
Long, long ago.

Sheep on the hillside lay
Whiter than snow;
Shepherds were watching them,
Long, long ago.

Then from the happy sky,
Angels bent low,
Singing their songs of joy,
Long, long ago.

For in a manger bed,
Cradled we know,
Christ came to Bethlehem,
Long, long ago.

Anon.

Away in a Manger

Away in a manger,
No crib for a bed,
The little Lord Jesus
Laid down his sweet head.
The stars in the bright sky
Look'd down where he lay,
The little Lord Jesus
Asleep on the hay.

The cattle are lowing,
The baby awakes,
But little Lord Jesus
No crying he makes.
I love thee, Lord Jesus,
Look down from the sky,
And stay by my cradle
Till morning is nigh.

Be near me, Lord Jesus,
I ask thee to stay
Close by me for ever,
And love me, I pray.
Bless all the dear children
In thy tender care,
And fit us for heaven,
To live with thee there.

Anon.

In the Stable: Christmas Haiku

Donkey
My long ears can hear
Angels singing, but my song
Would wake the baby.

Dog
I will not bark but
Lie, head on paws, eyes watching
All these visitors.

Cat
I'll wash my feet. For
This baby all should be clean.
My purr will soothe him.

Owl
My round eyes look down.
No starlit hunting this night:
Peace to little ones!

Spider
My fine web sparkles:
Indoor star in the roof's night
Over the baby.

Michael Harrison

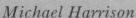

The Shepherds' Carol

We stood on the hills, Lady,
Our day's work done,
Watching the frosted meadows
That winter had won.

The evening was calm, Lady,
The air so still,
Silence more lovely than music
Folded the hill.

There was a star, Lady,
Shone in the night,
Larger than Venus it was
And bright, so bright.

Oh, a voice from the sky, Lady,
It seemed to us then
Telling of God being born
In the world of men.

And so we have come, Lady,
Our day's work done,
Our love, our hopes, ourselves
We give to your son.

Anon.

61

I Wish I'd Been Present at Christmas Past

I wish I'd been a shepherd
and heard the angels sing.
I wish I'd been to Bethlehem
and seen the Infant King.

I wish I'd been a wise man
at the stable bare
following the star with
gold, frankincense, and myrrh.

I wish I'd been an animal
who shared my manger hay
with that special newborn baby
on that first Christmas Day.

Paul Cookson

Rock-a-bye

Rock-a-bye, baby
The world is your cradle,
The wind only blows
If you speak the word,
Angels will rock you
And sing to God's glory,
The message of peace
And goodwill shall be heard.

Rock-a-bye, baby
The stars are your baubles,
Crafted by you
Then set into space,
Born into weakness
You travel beside us,
Showing us life
In your beautiful face.

Daphne Kitching

I Saw Three Ships

I saw three ships come sailing by,
On Christmas Day, on Christmas Day,
I saw three ships come sailing by,
On Christmas Day in the morning.

And who was in those ships all three,
On Christmas Day, on Christmas Day,
And who was in those ships all three,
On Christmas Day in the morning?

Our Saviour Christ and his Lady,
On Christmas Day, on Christmas Day,
Our Saviour Christ and his Lady,
On Christmas Day in the morning.

Oh! They sailed into Bethlehem,
On Christmas Day, on Christmas Day.
Oh! They sailed into Bethlehem,
On Christmas Day in the morning.

And all the bells on earth did ring,
On Christmas Day, on Christmas Day,
And all the bells on earth did ring,
On Christmas Day in the morning.

Anon.

A Christmas Legend

Three trees shivered
in the cold moonshine,
a date palm, an olive,
and a dark green pine.

They whispered together,
saw a light in the sky,
paused, secrets forgotten,
heard a new baby's cry.

They stood in the yard
near the child's manger bed.
'What can we give him?'
the gentle pine said.

The olive gave oil
to soothe his small feet.
The palm promised dates,
all sticky and sweet.

'But what about me?'
the poor pine tree cried.
'I can't think of a thing.
I've tried and I've tried!'

Hearing her cries all
the stars tumbled down
to light up her branches
like a bright golden crown.

Then the pine tree stood tall
so the baby could see
on that first Christmas Day,
his first Christmas tree.

Moira Andrew

Christmas Wishes

A
star
shining,
angels singing,
snow shimmering,
two shepherds watching,
three proud kings travelling,
in a stable, a newborn baby crying,
in deep forests, silvery trees sparkling,
in high church towers, sweet bells chiming,
in busy streets, tinsel swaying, lights gleaming,
tambourines shaking, drums beating, trumpets blaring,
at home, mince pies baking, plum puddings steaming,
fat turkeys crackling, champagne bubbling,
the glad green tree, lights glistening,
Christmas greetings winging
across
frosty
winter
skies.

Moira Andrew

Christmas in the Sun

Singing carols by the sea
Eating turkey on the sands
Paper hats, mince pies, and crackers
This is Christmas in hot lands.

Candlelight in cooler evenings
Christmas dinner out of doors
Summer flowers as decorations
Carnivals for Santa Claus.

Santa Claus may have his reindeer
And he still might come by sleigh
But he has been seen on surfboard
Skimming over warm sea spray.

Children from these warmer countries
Never see a flake of snow
But the flickering lights of fireworks
Set their Christmas night aglow.

For this season for all people
Whether near or from afar
Is a time of celebration
Remembering a special star.

Brenda Williams

Christmas Morning

The stockings hanging on the beds
were thin last night, now fat instead.
It's still quite dark, but children creep
down the stairs, all half asleep.
Shapes that they can hardly see
lie underneath the Christmas tree,
exciting shapes, some big, some small,
mysterious objects, wall to wall.
Then there's rustling paper, creaks and bumps,
happy cries and muffled thumps
and Mum and Dad wake up and yawn.
'It's dark!' they groan. 'Not even dawn.'
But downstairs children laugh and play
at 5a.m. on Christmas Day.

Marian Swinger

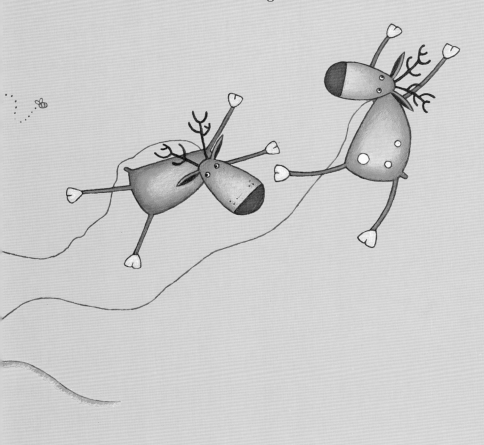

Horace's Christmas Disappointment

Young Horace Giraffe on Christmas Eve
Put out his stocking to receive
Whatever Santa Claus might bring.
You may indeed be wondering
What sort of size such stockings are,
Since even small giraffes are far
Bigger than quite a tall man is.
Young Horace Giraffe had measured his,
And found it stretched four feet or so
From ample top to roomy toe.

What piles and piles of presents he
Imagined packed there presently!
A hundred tangerines; a bunch
Of ripe bananas for his lunch;
Five watermelons; fifty figs;
The most delicious juicy sprigs
Plucked from the tops of special trees
With leaves as sweet as honey-bees;
And in the very bottom, some
Chocolates full of candied rum.

Alas, poor Horace! Christmas Day
Dawned, and he rose from where he lay
To snatch the stocking from the bed—
But though it bulged, he felt with dread
How light it was . . . He reached inside—

The size of Horace, was a SCARF
(A useful garment, yes, I know,
But oh, it was a bitter blow.)
The scarf was fully ten yards long,
And striped and bright and very strong.
It filled the stocking, top to toe,
And Horace was quite filled with woe.

The moral is: *A USEFUL* PRESENT
IN STOCKINGS IS RATHER
SELDOM PLEASANT.

Anthony Thwaite

Edible Angels

You can talk of hot roast turkey
   with skin that's golden brown.
You can pray for Christmas pudding
   with cream that dribbles down.

You can murmur on for warm mince pies
   that crumble as you bite.
But for me there is one special thing
   I think of with delight.

You can dream of hot potatoes
   and steaming sprouts, of course.
You can sing of dark, rich gravy
   and scrumptious, thick bread sauce.

But, when it comes to Christmas,
   the things that sing to me
are the little chocolate angels
   that swing upon the tree.

Tony Mitton

For fifty weeks I've languished
Upon the cupboard shelf,
Forgotten and uncared for,
I've muttered to myself.
But now the year is closing
And Christmastime is here,
They dust me down and tell me
To show a little cheer.
Between the plaster snowman
And little glassy lake

They stand me in the middle
Of some ice-covered cake,
And for a while there's laughter,
But as the week wears on,
They cut up all the landscape
Till every scrap is gone.
Then with the plaster snowman
And little lake of glass
I'm banished to the cupboard
For one more year to pass.

Colin West

73

Auntie Mimi's Mistletoe

Auntie Mimi's mistletoe,
She ties it to her head
And goes round kissing everyone,
She's kissed my uncle Fred,
She's kissed my mum, she's kissed my dad,
The postman, and the cat,
She kissed the man next door so hard
She squashed his glasses flat,
She's kissed my little brother,
Though he hid behind the tree,
And now she's coming my way
But she won't get me!

Richard Edwards

Hold Tight!

It's like I told you . . .
A Christmas cracker depends
On who's holding the ends.
If you don't give a hard jerk
It won't work.
You hold it so—
You don't let go.
A quick, firm tug,
A sudden crack!
It's all so simple
When you know the knack.
What's in the middle?
I'm coming to that:
Just a funny old riddle
And a paper hat.

Max Fatchen

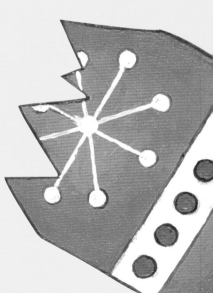

It Started With a Baby

It started with a Baby
and a manger, soft with hay.
It started with three Kings
who came from far away.
It started with some shepherds
who saw angels, tall and bright.
It started with a brilliant star
which filled the skies with light.
Now Christmas trees are sparkling
and the shops are filled with toys
which will shortly be delivered
to happy girls and boys.
Toddlers wait for Father Christmas
with his reindeer and his sleigh,
Christmas cards are posted
and, on Christmas Day,
there's the opening of the presents
and the Christmas games and fun,
but, later on, at bedtime
when Christmas Day is done
remember how it started,
with a Baby, in the hay,
in a manger, in a stable,
two thousand years away.

Marian Swinger

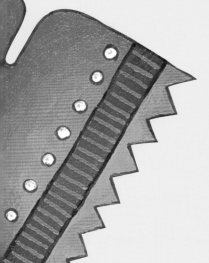

We three
kings of
Orient
are...

We Three Kings

We three kings of Orient are;
Bearing gifts we traverse afar,
Field and fountain, moor and mountain,
Following yonder star.

O star of wonder, star of night,
Star with royal beauty bright,
Westward leading, still proceeding,
Guide us to thy perfect light.

Melchior:

Born a king on Bethlehem plain,
Gold I bring, to crown him again,
King forever, ceasing never,
Over us all to reign.

Caspar:

Frankincense to offer have I,
Incense owns a deity nigh;
Prayer and praising, all men raising,
Worship him, God most high.

Balthazar:

Myrrh is mine; its bitter perfume
Breathes a life of gathering gloom;
Sorrowing, sighing, bleeding, dying,
Sealed in the stone-cold tomb.

All:

Glorious now behold him arise,
King and God and sacrifice,
Alleluia, alleluia,
Earth to the heav'ns replies.

Traditional

The Gift

Gold, frankincense, and myrrh,
three precious things,
were given to a baby
by three kings
while one great, glorious star
shone high above.
The baby's gift to all,
beyond price, was love.

Marian Swinger

Carol of the Brown King

Of the three Wise Men
Who came to the King,
One was a brown man,
So they sing.

Of the three Wise Men
Who followed the Star,
One was a brown king
From afar.

They brought fine gifts
Of spices and gold
In jewelled boxes
Of beauty untold.

Unto His humble
Manger they came
And bowed their heads
In Jesus' name.

Three Wise Men,
One dark like me—
Part of His
Nativity.

Langston Hughes

Winter Song

Silver white
Is the world tonight
As we follow the star
That burns so bright.

Golden light
Points the way
To a child who sleeps
On a bed of hay.

Jewelled bright
On the stable floor
Are the gifts we leave
On the shining straw.

Icy white
Is the sifting snow
That covers our tracks
As we homeward go.

Cynthia Rider

The Christmas Donkey

I am the donkey who saw it all.
   I saw the couple come—
Joseph and Mary wrapped in a shawl—
   And the birth of their tiny son.

I warmed the baby with my hot breath
   While the night grew cold and sharp.
As He smiled at me from His bed of straw
   Light shone round His head in the dark.

And a stream of visitors came to my stable
   Guided by a bright star
And angels who sang of peace to all people
   Wherever, whoever, they are.

But the animals were not forgotten;
   Blessed and happy were we
To be first at the birth of the Holy Child
   And to stay with His family.

I am the donkey who saw it all—
   I saw the shepherds come
And three Wise Men, with their gifts of gold
   For the baby born in my home.

Mal Lewis Jones

A Christmas Tree is for Christmas not for Ever

Nobody wants a Christmas tree after Christmas.
Nobody wants a tree that's lost its looks.
Nobody wants a tree without a star on top.
Nobody wants to bother about its roots.

Nobody wants tired tinsel after Christmas.
Nobody wants the mistletoe hanging there.
Nobody wants torn wrapping paper either.
Nobody wants to find holly on their chair.

Nobody wants the tree without its needles.
Nobody wants the fairy with her wings all bent.
Nobody wants to start the basic clearing up.
Nobody wants to remember where things went.

Nobody wants to remember that twelfth night's here.
Nobody wants to take the baubles off the tree.
Nobody wants to put the cards away . . . but . . .
Everybody's going to help before they get their tea!

Janis Priestley

Another Christmas Gone

The first white hill still glistens
Beneath the moonlit skies;
As on the night of Christmas
Untrod it sleeping lies.
A new born year is waiting
To meet the early dawn;
And whisper this to all the world,
Another Christmas gone.

Anon.

Three Christmas Wishes

If I had three Christmas wishes
My first wish would be
For an end to hunger and poverty.

If I had three Christmas wishes
My second would be for
An end to violence, hatred, and war.

If I had three Christmas wishes
My third wish would be
That we take proper care of the land and the sea.

John Foster

Ring Out, Wild Bells

Ring out, wild bells, to the wild sky,
   The flying cloud, the frosty light:
   The year is dying in the night;
Ring out, wild bells, and let him die.

Ring out the old, ring in the new,
   Ring happy bells, across the snow:
   The year is going, let him go;
Ring out the false, ring in the true.

Alfred, Lord Tennyson

Index of Titles and First Lines

(First lines are in italics)

Acknowledgements

Moira Andrew: 'Christmas Wishes', copyright © Moira Andrew 2001, first published in *Ready to Go: Ideas for Christmas* (Scholastic, 2001), reprinted by permission of the author; **Ann Bonner**: 'Angels', copyright © Ann Bonner 1999, first published in Jill Bennett (ed.): *Christmas Poems* (OUP, 1999), reprinted by permission of the author; **Charles Causley**: 'High in the Heaven' from *The Gift of a Lamb* (Robson Books, 1978), reprinted by permission of David Higham Associates; **Stanley Cook**: 'Christmas Cards' first published in *The Poem Box* (Blackie, 1991), and 'Christmas Trees', from *Selected Poems* (Peterloo, 1981), both copyright © The Estate of Stanley Cook, reprinted by permission of Sarah Matthews; **Sue Cowling**: 'Reindeer Rap', copyright © Sue Cowling 2001, first published in John Foster (ed.): *Ready, Steady, Rap* (OUP, 2001), reprinted by permission of the author; **June Crebbin**: 'School Carol' from *The Jungle Sale* (Viking Kestrel, 1988), copyright © June Crebbin 1988, reprinted by permission of the author; **Richard Edwards**: 'Pilot' and 'If I Were Father Christmas' from *If Only* (Viking, 1990), copyright © Richard Edwards 1990; 'Carole Caroll' and 'Auntie Mimi's Mistletoe' from *Nonsense Christmas Rhymes* (OUP, 2002), copyright © Richard Edwards 2002; all reprinted by permission of the author; **Eleanor Farjeon**: 'The Children's Carol' from *Silver-Sand and Snow* (Michael Joseph, 1951), reprinted by permission of David Higham Associates; **Max Fatchen**: 'Carol Singers' and 'Hold Tight!', copyright © Max Fatchen 2003, first published in this collection by permission of John Johnson (Authors' Agent) Ltd; **John Foster**: 'Three Christmas Wishes' from *Making Waves* (OUP, 1997), copyright © John Foster 1997, and 'Advent Calendar', copyright © John Foster 2001, first published in John Foster (ed.): *Rhyme Time: Around the Year* (OUP, 2001), reprinted by permission of the author; **Rose Fyleman**: 'December', reprinted by permission of The Society of Authors as the Literary Representative of the Estate of Rose Fyleman; **Michael Harrison**: 'In the Stable: Christmas Haiku' from *Junk Mail* (OUP, 1993), copyright © Michael Harrison 1993, reprinted by permission of the author; **Theresa Heine**: 'Christmas Star', copyright © Theresa Heine 1987, first published in John Foster (ed.): *Another First Poetry Book* (OUP, 1987), reprinted by permission of the author; **Langston Hughes**: 'Carol of the Brown King' from *The Collected Poems of Langston Hughes* (Knopf, 1994), reprinted by permission of David Higham Associates; **Mal Lewis Jones**: 'The Christmas Donkey', copyright © Mal Jones 2000, from Ivan and Mal Jones (eds.): *Good Night, Sleep Tight* (Scholastic, 2000), reprinted by permission of the author; **Jean Kenward**: 'Sir Winter', copyright © Jean Kenward 1999, first published in Alison Green (ed.): *The Macmillan Book of Christmas* (Macmillan, 1999), reprinted by permission of the author; **Patricia Leighton**: 'Coming for Christmas' and 'The Christmas Pudding — from Start to Finish!', copyright © Patricia Leighton 2000, first published in Paul Cookson (ed.): *Christmas Poems* (Macmillan, 2000), reprinted by permission of the author; **A. A. Milne**: 'The More it Snows' from *The House at Pooh Corner* (Methuen, 1928), copyright © A. A. Milne 1928, reprinted by permission of the publisher, Egmont Books Ltd, London; **Judith Nicholls**: 'Christmas Eve' from *Higgledy Piggledy* (Mary Glasgow Publications, 1990), copyright © Judith Nicholls 1990, reprinted by permission of the author; **Janis Priestley**: 'A Christmas Tree is for Christmas Not for Ever', copyright © Janis Priestley 1998, first published in Brian Moses (ed.): *We Three Kings* (Macmillan, 1998), reprinted by permission of the author; **Ruth Sawyer**: 'Words from an Old Spanish Carol' retitled 'Christmas Morn' from *The Long Christmas* (Viking Penguin, 1941), copyright 1941 by Ruth Sawyer, reprinted by permission of Pollinger Ltd and Viking Penguin, an imprint of Penguin Putnam Books for Young Readers, a division of Penguin Putnam, Inc. All rights reserved; **Laurence Smith**: 'Christmas Tree', copyright © Laurence Smith 1983, first published in M. Harrison & C. Stuart-Clark (eds.): *The Oxford Book of Christmas Poems* (OUP, 1983), reprinted by permission of the author; **Anthony Thwaite**: 'Horace's Christmas Disappointment', copyright © Anthony Thwaite 1982, first published in *Allsorts 5* (Macmillan, 1982), reprinted by permission of the author; **Steve Turner**: 'December 19' from *Dad, You're Not Funny* (Lion Publishing, 1999), copyright © Steve Turner 1999, reprinted by permission of the publishers; **Colin West**: 'Parcels' from *Between the Sun, the Moon and Me* (Hutchinson, 1990), copyright © Colin West 1990, and 'The Father Christmas on the Cake' from *A Moment in Rhyme* (Hutchinson, 1987), copyright © Colin West 1987, reprinted by permission of the author.

Illustrations by:

Mark Marshall

16–17, 28–9, 34–5, 44–5, 50–1, 56–7, 58–9, 66–7, 83, 84–5.

Melanie Williamson

Endpapers (front and back), title pages, contents pages, 14–15, 18–19, 22–3, 24–5, 30–1, 33, 36–7, 38–9, 40–1, 42–3, 46–7, 48–9, 54–5, 60–1, 64–5, 68–9, 72–3, 74–5, 76–7, 78–9, 80–1, 82, 86–7, Index of Titles and First Lines.

Joanne Partis

12–13, 20–1, 26–7, 52–3, 62–3, 70–1, 88–9.

...and a

HAPPY Ne